NATIONAL GEOGRAPHIC

Ladders

NIAGARA FALLS
AMERICAN WONDERS

T0308468

2 Mist-ified: My Very Wet Trip to Niagara Falls *First-Person Narrative*
by Debbie Nevins

10 Niagara Falls On the Move *Science Article*
by Jennifer A. Smith

18 Thunder Speaks *Legend*
by Elizabeth Massie, illustrated by Craig Phillips

26 Over the Falls! *Narrative*
by David Holford

32 Discuss

Mist-ified

by Debbie Nevins

My Very Wet Trip to Niagara Falls

CANADA

Niagara Falls

UNITED STATES

There are many places to view the power of Niagara Falls. At Prospect Point, we saw the American Falls.

Hi! I'm Jacob. I'm visiting Niagara Falls with my family. It is the most powerful waterfall in North America. We are in Niagara Falls, New York. There are two cities with the same name. They are on each side of the Niagara River. One is Niagara Falls, New York. The other is Niagara Falls, Ontario, in Canada. The falls themselves are named Niagara Falls. It can be confusing!

Niagara Falls is actually three waterfalls. The largest one is in Canada. The other two are in the United States. They're all located on the Niagara River, which connects Lake Erie and Lake Ontario and marks the **international** border between Canada and the United States.

Here's one of the Maid of the Mist boats that travel past Niagara Falls.

Today we're going to ride on one of the famous Maid of the Mist boats. These boats bring visitors so close to the falls that they can feel the spray and mist from the water. My sister Lili says that when we get that close to the falls, I'm going to get "Mist-ified." I have no idea what that means. She won't tell me, and I'm getting worried. I hope it isn't scary!

The Blue Poncho

We're waiting to get our tickets for the Maid of the Mist ferryboat tour. I remember a story about the falls. It's a Native American tale about the Thunder Spirit, who controls the falls and sends the mist up to the sky to be clouds. Maybe that is what Lili means when she says "Mist-ified." There's some scary stuff in the tale, too, but I know it's just a story. As we stand in line on the Canadian side,

We saw lots of people enjoying the American Falls in their blue ponchos.

We noticed that the people returning from the Maid of the Mist tour were soaked. Are we going to get that wet?

ATTRACTION SINCE 1

4

everyone puts on a blue poncho. A poncho is sort of a raincoat with a hood. There are hundreds of us waiting to get on the ferry. We look like a bunch of Little Blue Riding Hoods. Lili and I see people coming off another one of the boats. They are wet, but they sure look happy.

I forget about being nervous until my sister says, "Ha, ha. They all got Mist-ified." I ask Mom what *mystified* means. She says it means confused. But the people getting off the boat don't look confused at all. They just look wet. I'm starting to feel confused myself.

Roaring Waters

I'm standing on the deck of the Maid of the Mist close to the front of the boat. We ride out into calm waters. The powerful engines shake the deck beneath my feet. My heart is pounding like crazy. Am I scared or just excited?

Our boat floats first to the American Falls. There we hear a rumbling roar. The water spills 180 feet down and hits huge boulders at the base of the falls, sending up large clouds of mist. Less than 10 percent of the Niagara River's water falls over this section. The rest of it goes over the Canadian Falls. The boulders in the river keep our boat from getting too close. I don't know why we need these ponchos. We barely feel a drop.

Next, we ride by a smaller **cascade** called Bridal Veil Falls. On an island near its base, I see people in yellow ponchos. Mom calls them "yellow jackets." They are taking the Cave of the Winds tour. You used to be able to walk behind the falls into a cave, but the cave collapsed years ago. Today people walk just a few feet away from the falls. Maybe we can do that after our boat tour.

We spotted a long line of people wearing yellow ponchos climbing a stairway. They were on the Cave of the Winds tour. The Hurricane Deck at the top stands only 20 feet from Bridal Veil Falls!

HURRICANE DECK

As we got closer to the falls, everybody wanted to take a picture.

Wall of Water

We ride closer to Horseshoe Falls. The air grows cooler and the fog becomes thicker. The roar sounds like a train. No, it sounds like 100 trains! I start to shiver. "Hey Lili!" I yell. But she can't hear me. Everyone around me is laughing and cheering loudly. Many are taking pictures and videos.

We get so close to the falls that we are surrounded by white mist. I feel like I'm in the middle of a giant rainstorm. The other 90 percent of the Niagara River crashes down here!

As the boat turns, I can see the "horseshoe" shape of the falls. A rainbow hangs in the mist. The Native Americans believe this place is magical, and I think they are right. Lots of water moves very quickly over Niagara Falls. And all of that

From the observation deck, we noticed the green color of Horseshoe Falls. The color comes from very tiny pieces of plant and rock that mix with the water as it travels down the Niagara River.

pounding water breaks down the rocks underneath and then carries away the bits of rocks. This is called **erosion**. Erosion is wearing away the falls. But they won't be completely worn away for another 50,000 years. I'm glad that I had a chance to see this awesome sight.

As we get off of the boat, I catch up with my sister. We are soaking wet from the mist. "Hey Lili," I say. "I figured it out. Looks like we all got Mist-ified!"

Everybody on the Maid of the Mist got "Mist-ified" that day. This may be the first time I ever figured out one of my sister Lili's jokes!

Check In   What sights did Jacob see from the Maid of the Mist?

9

Niagara Falls
On the Move

by Jennifer A. Smith

Rushing water, a loud roar, and misty rainbows—all of these await you at Niagara Falls. Where did all of this water come from? Where is it all going?

> From high above, you can see the rushing water of the Niagara River tumble over the rocky cliffs. Two large waterfalls and one smaller waterfall make up Niagara Falls.

About 750,000 gallons of water rush over Niagara Falls each second.

Carved by Ice

Niagara Falls formed more than ten thousand years ago. Ice was very important to its creation. An **ice age** is a period of time when thick ice sheets covered large areas of Earth. During the most recent ice age, ice sheets about one-and-a-half miles thick covered much of North America. This included the area around Niagara Falls.

These large ice sheets slowly moved south. They dug a **basin**, or hollowed-out land. It was like scooping ice cream out of a container. This area later became the Great Lakes.

As the ice sheets melted, they left behind a huge amount of water. This water filled the basin, creating the Great Lakes. The water also formed the Niagara River. Water from the river fell over a steep cliff. This is now known as Niagara Falls.

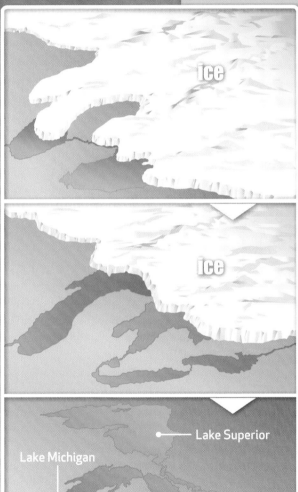

Lake Superior
Lake Michigan
Lake Huron
Niagara Falls
Lake Erie
Lake Ontario

This diagram shows how moving ice sheets formed the Great Lakes and the Niagara River. This process took thousands of years.

The Three Falls

Millions of people come to see the three waterfalls on the Niagara River. They visit the American side and Canadian side. The American Falls and Bridal Veil Falls are part of the United States. Most of Horseshoe Falls lies in Canada.

With thousands of gallons of water rushing over three waterfalls, the roar at Niagara Falls can be deafening. But what if the water stopped? Late in the evening of March 29, 1848, a strange thing happened. The falls went silent. For at least 30 hours, ice far upstream blocked the river's water flow. The falls became just a couple of drips of water. On March 31, there was a loud crack. The ice broke up. Rushing water flowed back over the falls again.

American Falls

American Falls is 190 feet tall. It is a little taller than Horseshoe Falls. American Falls is only 1,060 feet wide. That's less than half as wide as Horseshoe Falls.

Horseshoe Falls

Horseshoe Falls is 185 feet tall and 2,200 feet wide. That makes it about as tall as an 18-story building. It is much larger than American Falls.

Bridal Veil Falls

Bridal Veil Falls is the smallest of the falls. It is 56 feet wide. Visitors who take the Cave of the Winds tour get an up-close view of Bridal Veil Falls.

Wearing Away

The cliffs where Niagara Falls tumble used to be seven miles from where they are today. For thousands of years, the falls have been slowly moving up the Niagara River. The spot where the water crashes down onto the rocks at the foot of the falls has been changing. The powerful water breaks up this soft rock. This creates a deep passage, or **gorge**. As a result, there is nothing to hold up the rock that the water flows over. This rock collapses, the falls move farther up the river, and the gorge gets longer.

At one point, the falls were moving up the river as much as six feet per year. However, engineers have slowed down the water flow. This has kept the falls from moving as quickly. One way they have done this is by building tunnels. Some of the water from the Niagara River flows into the tunnels. This way, not all of it flows over the falls. When less water goes over the falls, erosion slows down. Now the falls move up the river only about one foot per year.

river

This diagram shows the movement of Niagara Falls up the Niagara River over the years as erosion wears the rocky cliffs away.

2007

1886

1842

1819

1764

1678

gorge

Check In How did tremendous ice sheets help to form the falls?

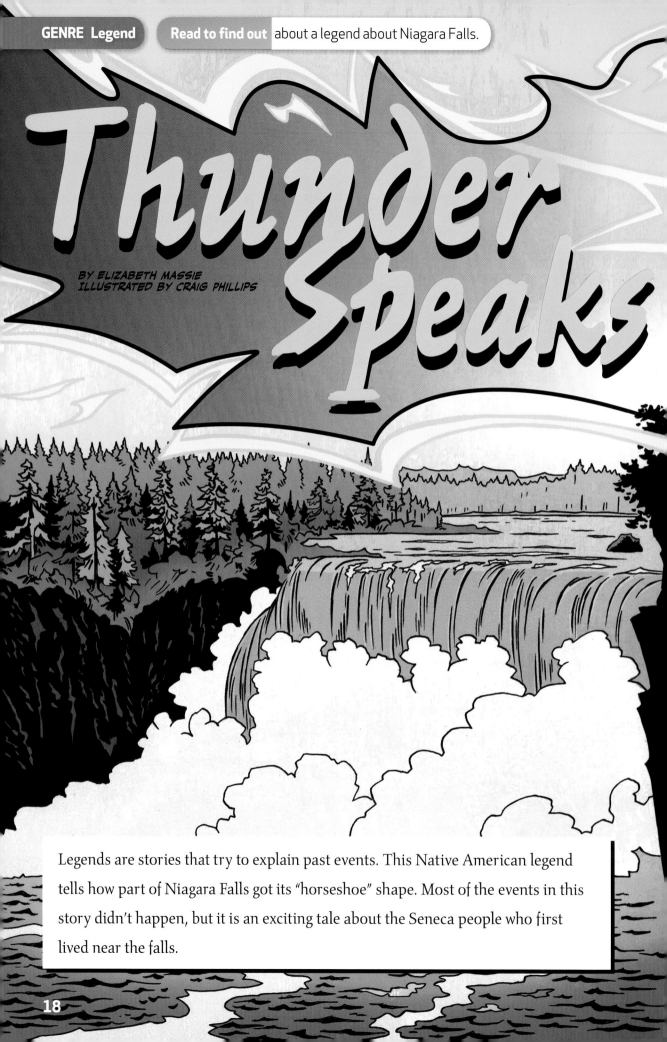

Thunder Speaks

BY ELIZABETH MASSIE
ILLUSTRATED BY CRAIG PHILLIPS

Legends are stories that try to explain past events. This Native American legend tells how part of Niagara Falls got its "horseshoe" shape. Most of the events in this story didn't happen, but it is an exciting tale about the Seneca people who first lived near the falls.

LONG AGO, THE PEOPLE OF A SENECA VILLAGE WERE SUFFERING. THEIR CROPS WERE DYING, AND MANY PEOPLE WERE ILL. A YOUNG VILLAGE GIRL WAS VERY WORRIED.

SO MANY LIVING THINGS IN OUR VILLAGE ARE SICK, BUT WHAT CAN WE DO?

I DO NOT KNOW, DEAR CHILD. WE HAVE CAREFULLY PLANTED AND WATERED OUR CROPS, BUT THEY WILL NOT GROW ANYMORE. WE HAVE ALSO TAKEN GOOD CARE OF OUR PEOPLE, BUT MANY ARE SICK AND HUNGRY.

THE YOUNG GIRL WENT TO SWIM IN A CAVE NEAR THE FALLS. SWIMMING CALMED HER. SHE TRIED TO THINK OF WAYS TO HELP HER VILLAGE.

SHE WAS FLOATING IN THE WATER WHEN A SNAKE SLID FROM BEHIND A ROCK.

FRIGHTENED, THE YOUNG GIRL RAN FROM THE CAVE. SHE SLIPPED AND FELL INTO THE NIAGARA RIVER. SHE WAS SWEPT AWAY BY THE FAST WATER.

SOMEONE HELP ME!

I'VE FALLEN INTO THE RAPIDS!

SHE TRIED TO SWIM TO THE SHORE. BUT THE WATER CARRIED THE YOUNG GIRL TO THE WATERFALL. SHE TUMBLED OVER THE EDGE. AS SHE FELL, A MIST BEGAN TO RISE AROUND HER. THE MIST SAVED HER LIFE.

I'M NOT HURT! THE MIST CAUGHT ME AND HELPED ME TO SAFETY.

SHE QUICKLY CLIMBED OUT OF THE WATER. SHE WAS HAPPY TO BE ON DRY LAND AGAIN.

THUNDER SPIRIT EXPLAINED THAT FAMINE IS A TIME WHEN THERE IS VERY LITTLE FOOD. HE TOLD HER THAT THE FAMINE SPIRIT IS A SNAKE SPIRIT THAT DESTROYS CROPS AND MAKES PEOPLE GO HUNGRY. HE HAD BEEN SWIMMING IN THE LAKE NEAR THE YOUNG GIRL'S VILLAGE. HE WAS POISONING THE WATER THE VILLAGERS USED ON THEIR CROPS.

THUNDER SPIRIT TOLD THE YOUNG GIRL TO RETURN TO HER VILLAGE. SHE HAD TO TELL HER PEOPLE THAT THE WATER WAS POISONED AND THAT THEY HAD TO MOVE UPRIVER TO ESCAPE FAMINE SPIRIT.

WE MUST MOVE UP THE RIVER AND BUILD A NEW VILLAGE.

WITH THE WORDS OF THUNDER SPIRIT STILL RINGING IN HER EARS, THE YOUNG GIRL RUSHED BACK TO HER VILLAGE. SHE TOLD HER PEOPLE TO LEAVE. THE MEN GATHERED UP THEIR BOWS AND ARROWS AND CANOES. THE WOMEN HELPED THEIR CHILDREN PACK UP THEIR THINGS. MOTHERS CARRIED THEIR BABIES ON THEIR BACKS.

THE VILLAGERS TRAVELED UPRIVER IN THEIR CANOES. THEY LOOKED FOR LAND FOR A NEW VILLAGE. BUT FAMINE SPIRIT SAW THEM LEAVE AND FOLLOWED QUIETLY.

AFTER MANY HOURS OF PADDLING, THE SENECA CHIEF CHOSE A SPOT FOR A NEW VILLAGE.

AS THE PEOPLE SET UP THEIR NEW VILLAGE, THE YOUNG GIRL WENT TO COLLECT FIREWOOD. SHE WAS GATHERING TWIGS WHEN THUNDER SPIRIT CAME TO HER.

THUNDER SPIRIT EXPLAINED THAT FAMINE SPIRIT HAD FOLLOWED THE YOUNG GIRL'S PEOPLE TO THIS PLACE. HE WOULD HARM THE NEW VILLAGE AND RUIN THE CROPS IF SOMEONE COULDN'T STOP HIM.

THE SENECA PEOPLE LIKED THEIR NEW VILLAGE. THE YOUNG GIRL STILL WORRIED THAT FAMINE SPIRIT WAS NEARBY. BUT SHE KEPT HER FEARS TO HERSELF.

WHEN MORNING CAME, THE FIGHT WAS OVER. FAMINE SPIRIT WAS DEAD. THUNDER SPIRIT HAD RETURNED TO HIS CAVE. BUT EVERYONE COULD SEE WHERE THE BATTLE HAD TAKEN PLACE. THE TWO FIGHTING SPIRITS HAD RESHAPED THE LAND AND THE FALLS.

THE EDGE OF THE FALLS, WHICH HAD BEEN STRAIGHT, WAS NOW BENT INTO THE SHAPE OF A HORSESHOE.

THE VILLAGERS STOOD BESIDE THE WATERFALL. THEY SAW HOW ITS EDGE WAS NOW CURVED. THEY CELEBRATED BECAUSE FAMINE SPIRIT WOULDN'T BE COMING BACK.

THE ELDERS OF MY VILLAGE SAY I SHALL BE REMEMBERED FOREVER!

THANK YOU, THUNDER SPIRIT, FOR PROTECTING US!

FAMINE SPIRIT WAS GONE. THE SENECA COULD ONCE AGAIN GROW HEALTHY CROPS. THE VILLAGE AND ITS PEOPLE GREW STRONG. AND WHAT BECAME OF THE YOUNG GIRL? HER PEOPLE WERE GRATEFUL. TO HONOR HER, THEY NAMED HER THE MAID OF THE MIST.

Check In How does this legend explain the current shape of the falls?

OVER THE FALLS!

by David Holford

For more than 150 years, people have tried risky feats at Niagara Falls. Some have plunged over the falls, trying to make it through the powerful whirlpool and rapids below. Others have walked on tightropes across the river. They are **daredevils**, people who seek adventure by risking their lives. Some Niagara Falls daredevils have survived. Sadly, others have not. Here are some stories of those who have lived to tell about their wild feats.

ANNIE EDSON TAYLOR
HEROINE OF NIAGARA FALLS
OCT 24 1901
F.M. RUSSELL Mgr.

The first person to go over Niagara Falls was 63-year-old schoolteacher Annie Taylor. She did it in a wooden barrel in 1901. She hoped the stunt would make her rich and famous. For a few years, she earned money by taking photographs with tourists. She didn't become rich. But she will definitely live on in history.

A small boat carried Taylor and her barrel to the middle of the river. Helpers put the barrel into the water near Horseshoe Falls. She would have had a shorter drop at American Falls. But it would have been a rougher ride. There's little chance someone could survive a landing there. The base of American Falls has many pointed rocks.

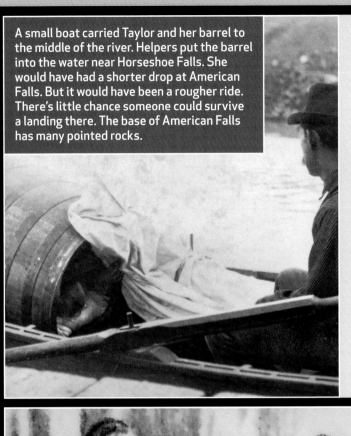

A harness held Taylor inside the barrel. The barrel was stuffed with pillows for padding. Even with the pillows, she was slammed around in the rapids. Dropping over the falls left her bruised and beaten.

Taylor's barrel was dragged to shore. Taylor was dazed as she was helped from the barrel. She said that nobody should ever do it again. In spite of her warning, her success made other daredevils want to try.

TAKING THE PLUNGE

Copycats soon followed Taylor. They took the plunge in many different devices. These included a large rubber ball and a barrel wrapped in inner tubes. Over time, the devices improved. Others faced the falls in barrels that were stronger and safer. But going over Niagara Falls was still risky and expensive. Now it is illegal to try to go over the falls. Today, the fine for breaking this law is $10,000.

In 1911, Bobby Leach went over the falls in this steel barrel. He survived but spent weeks in the hospital with injuries. He was still using a cane when this photo was taken.

William Hill didn't go over the falls in his barrel. Instead, he used it for a trip through the unsafe rapids below the falls. His first attempt was in the 1930s. He was swirling in the waters for hours before he was rescued. In his second attempt, the barrel began to leak. His son swam close enough to the rapids to throw him a rope and save his life.

In 1984, Karel Soucek became the eighth person to survive the falls. He went over them in this barrel of lightweight metal and plastic. He escaped major injuries. But authorities took his barrel and fined him $500!

In 1995, Steve Trotter and Lori Martin went over the falls together. They used this metal barrel covered with a strong but lightweight material. As a result of their stunt, Trotter and Martin spent several days in jail. Trotter later apologized to rescue workers who risked their lives to pull him and Martin from the rapids.

Peter DeBernardi and Jeffrey Petkovich were the first to go over the falls together. They used this bright yellow steel barrel for their plunge in 1989.

THE GREAT BLONDIN:
Tightrope Walker

In 1859, a circus performer called "The Great Blondin" was the first person to cross the river's gorge on a tightrope. During his walk, Blondin sat on the rope. He lowered an empty bottle on a string into the gorge. He filled it with water, pulled it back up, and drank the water. Later, he did a backwards somersault on the tightrope.

Blondin gave several more shows, drawing crowds as large as 25,000 people. His act included bicycling on a rope high above the gorge. He would also walk the rope blindfolded. Once, he even carried a man across on his back!

By 1896, several more daredevils crossed the gorge on tightropes. After that, tightrope walks were banned, until an amazing event 116 years later.

The Great Blondin did many acts up on his wire. One time, he pushed a wheelbarrow across the rope.

A MODERN-DAY DAREDEVIL

In 2012, officials gave famous high-wire performer Nik Wallenda permission to do an even more risky stunt. He would walk across the gorge and over the falls. They wanted to increase **tourism** to help local businesses.

About 100,000 people came to watch the event. Millions more watched on television. The TV network made Wallenda wear a harness. It attached him to the wire in case he fell. Wallenda was 200 feet above the water where the cold spray and winds hit him. He carefully moved along. As he neared the Canadian side, the huge crowd cheered. Wallenda raised his fist in the air and ran the rest of the way. "The impossible is not so impossible if you set your mind to it," he said after his walk. "Reach for the skies and never give up!"

Nik Wallenda crossed over Horseshoe Falls on June 15, 2012. He went from the American side to the Canadian side. He walked on a wire that was as long as six football fields.

Check In   Who were two of the earliest Niagara Falls daredevils and what did they do?

Discuss

1. Tell about some of the ways you think the four selections in this book are linked.

2. Describe what you feel was the most exciting part of Jacob's trip to Niagara Falls.

3. Explain how Niagara Falls has moved up the Niagara River over time. What causes the falls to move up the river?

4. Why do you think so many daredevils have attempted to plunge over Niagara Falls? How have these attempts affected the community near the falls?

5. What do you still want to know about the amazing sights and history of Niagara Falls?